-0 AUG 1976

HERTFORDSHIRE LIBRARY SERVICE

This book is due for return on or before the date shown. You
may extend its loan by bringing the book to the library or,
once only, by post or telephone, quoting the date of return,
the letter and number on the date card, if applicable, and the
information at the top of this label.

The loan of books in demand cannot be extended.

THE TRAMWAYS
OF FALKIRK

ALAN W. BROTCHIE

PUBLISHED BY THE N.B. TRACTION GROUP

60p

FIRST PUBLISHED 1975

© A. W. BROTCHIE 1975

COVER New Market Street, Falkirk, in 1906. The new tram is passing the Burgh Buildings and the South African War Memorial (before it was unveiled).

Printed by Crown Press (Keighley) Limited, Chapel Lane, Keighley, West Yorkshire

FOREWORD

It is intended that this study of one of Scotland's smaller tramway systems should form the first part of a comprehensive coverage of tramways and transport in the Forth Valley and Fife. Detailed histories are in preparation of the tramways in Stirling, Dunfermline, Kirkcaldy, and Wemyss. It is possible a further volume could deal with the multitude of small bus operators of the area, whose competitive tactics caused the eventual downfall of the small tramways.

Each of these tramway systems contributed to the pattern of urban growth in the area it served, and each fulfilled a useful service by transporting workers cheaply, and other travellers economically. None of the tramways survived the 1930s, and recourse has been made to contemporary sources for information. Many of the employees of the Companies involved have been contacted and their reminiscences recorded. In particular, the late W. Miller of Larbert was a fund of information on Falkirk trams and buses. A transport enthusiast, he spent his whole working life in transport, and encouraged and cajoled his work-mates to turn up their old photographs and memories. This work was made more complete by his assistance.

Others whose specialised knowledge is gratefully acknowledged include W. H. Bett, J. K. D. Blair, and J. H. Price. Photographs are reproduced by courtesy of the following: Falkirk Herald, J. J. Herd, Mustograph Agency, N.B. Traction Group and Parsons Peebles Ltd., also Turntable Publications (per D. L. G. Hunter).

The depot at Carmuirs photographed on the opening day. At the back can be seen two Brush cars being completed.

Introduction

Falkirk lies in Central Scotland, on the south side of the valley of the River Forth. It is almost midway between Edinburgh and Glasgow, being 25 miles from the former and 22 miles from the latter. It lies at the centre of Scotland's most varied industrial area.

Coal and iron brought the Industrial Revolution to the area, and the establishment in 1759 of the Carron Company's foundries began the long association of the town with the iron industry. Today, although the Carron Company remains, the emphasis has shifted, with the twentieth century petro-chemical developments at the port of Grangemouth playing an ever increasing part in the industrial growth of the area.

The town of Falkirk stands slightly elevated above the flood plains of the Forth, and the flat area between the town and the river has been the scene of many defensive struggles. The eastern end of the Antonine Wall, built by the Romans in the second century to resist the unwelcome attentions of unfriendly natives, passes nearby, and some earthworks can still be discerned. William Wallace fought on these level banks — but unsuccessfully — in 1298.

Its central location made Falkirk an important market town long before the coming of the Iron Masters, and by the early eighteenth century the Falkirk cattle trysts were the premier Scottish market for sales of black cattle.

The story of transport in the area is long and involved, from the early drove roads, through the railway era to the present motorway age, but one facet of local transport which was unique to Falkirk was its tramway system. Its gauge — 4ft 0in — was unmatched elsewhere in Scotland, and its circular main route caused many to compare it to a toy railway. This likeness is shared with one other Scottish transport curiosity — the Glasgow Subway — also on a circular track and also to the same unusual gauge. However, the Falkirk tram, modernised at great expense in the 1930s, has gone, but the Subway remains, and it is now to be rebuilt at great expense. Perhaps had the tramway survived from the clutches of rapacious bus owners it might today have been performing a valuable service — pollution-free, using electricity. Before considering the trams in detail, some background to the transport history of the area is necessary.

Early Local Transportation

The first attempt to provide an alternative to the very poor roads of the eighteenth century became necessary with the establishment of heavy industry. The Carron Company showed the way, when one of the first Scottish canals was built, leading right into their works, from a straightened and dredged stretch of the River Carron which gave access to the Forth.

This was soon followed by the construction, between 1768 and 1790, of the Forth and Clyde Canal. This could take coastal vessels of up to 8ft 9in draught, and passed through Bainsford, midway between Falkirk and Carron. In 1810 the Carron Company built a horse-worked railway, linking their works with the Bainsford basin of the canal. The Carron Company made extensive use of wagonways to link their collieries with the works, the earliest recorded of these being opened in 1766, running $2\frac{1}{4}$ miles to Kinnaird Colliery.

An interesting experiment in combining rail and canal was conducted in August 1839 when a single line of railway was laid near Lock 16 of the Forth and Clyde Canal. A small locomotive (the "Victoria", built by William Dodds at the Kipps works of the Monkland and Kirkintilloch Railway) was used to pull barges, both goods and passenger boats. Speeds of up to 17 mph were achieved, but although horse power produced only 2 mph on average, the experiment was abandoned. It is believed that the wash produced at these speeds caused too much erosion of the canal banks.

The first main line railway reached Falkirk in 1842, when a branch was opened from the Edinburgh and Glasgow Railway. Eventually the whole area was covered by a network of railways, but now few of these remain. The Carron Company's horse railway to Bainsford was disused after about 1860 when the works were connected to the railway network, but now none of this once extensive rail system remains.

The most significant recent development in local transport was the opening in 1973 of the M9 Motorway. This has halved the motoring time to Edinburgh, and when the westward link to Stirling is complete, will put Falkirk back into its historical position at Scotland's crossroads.

Motor Bus Service

By the late nineteenth century, Falkirk formed the nucleus of a number of sizeable villages of which Grahamston, Bainsford, Camelon and Laurieston were absorbed into the burgh in 1900. Villages close by, but outwith the burgh, included Larbert, Stenhousemuir, Carron, Carronshore, Grangemouth, Polmont, Maddiston, Redding and Bonnybridge. The population of Falkirk in 1893 was 23,000, and in the surrounding area it approached 55,000.

At a meeting held at Westquarter in April 1898 a group of prominent local businessmen decided to form a company to run cars for hire in the Falkirk district. Those present included Captain Fenton Livingston of Westquarter, J. C. Urquhart, D. B. Hamilton, and J. M. Burns, a solicitor, all of Falkirk. Capital was raised and an order placed with Stirling's Motor Carriages (Ltd.) for three cars for eight passengers at a cost of £355 each, to be delivered by 2nd May. This date was met, and the new Falkirk & District Motor Car Company Ltd. commenced operations on 2nd May 1898, on a route from New Market Street, Falkirk, to Stenhousemuir, every 30 minutes from 8.00 am. It was advertised that an occasional service would be run between Camelon and Laurieston, and that other routes would be opened as additional cars were purchased. The contemporary account of the opening stated that the cars were "of a neat and compact appearance and their speed and comfort satisfied the demands of the most fastidious on the question of transport". J. M. Burns acted as Secretary of the Company, while David B. Hamilton was Manager.

The cars were small Daimler wagonettes with 8-seat bodies, and were identical to vehicles used to open contemporary routes in the Glasgow and Lanarkshire areas. One of the Falkirk Company's vehicles survives in the collection of John Gibson & Sons and was for a time on exhibition in Edinburgh Corporation's Transport Museum.

With further vehicles, from 11th June the service was increased to cover what was later to become the tramway circle, Falkirk-Carron-Stenhousemuir-Larbert-Camelon-Falkirk, at approximately hourly intervals in both clockwise and anti-clockwise directions. For the round trip 6d was charged, which effectively priced out the working man whose wage was then around 4d per hour. Additional routes were run from Hope Street, Falkirk, to Bonnybridge twice daily, single fare 6d; from East High Street, Falkirk, to Polmont twice daily, single fare 4d; and from East High Street to Laurieston eight times daily, single fare 2d, but with a proviso that these routes could be discontinued on holidays when the cars were used for touring. By December 1898 the manager was William Dodds, and fares were quoted as Falkirk to Stenhousemuir 3d, with 1d stages at Bainsford Bridge and Carron Bridge; Falkirk to Larbert 3d, with a 2d stage to Camelon; circular trip 6d; Falkirk to Laurieston 2d single, 3d return, and a new route, Falkirk to Carronshore, 3d single. For the circular trip of 6¼ miles one hour was allowed.

The Company gave up business in 1900 following an action raised in the local Sheriff Court by a Mr Robert McGilchrist who had been summarily ejected from a yard in Bryson Street, Grahamston which he had on lease and where he carried on a lemonade manufacturing business, to allow the Motor Car Company to use it as a garage. The Sheriff found against the Company, whose appeal to the Sheriff-Principal was also defeated. The last record of the Company was the auction on 20th February 1901 of its effects, including thirteen Daimler wagonettes.

In addition to the Motor Car Company, many horse buses and brakes ran from Falkirk to the surrounding villages. In 1901 there were no less than 73 of these, varying from 7 to 36 seat capacity. Horse bus operators included McLaren Brothers and John Reid, both of whom ran to Stenhousemuir, also Borthwick and Wyse, both running to Camelon.

Tramway Preparations

Early in 1900 an approach was made by two Edinburgh tramway entrepreneurs to Falkirk Town Council and various adjacent local authorities to obtain the concession for tramway construction in the area. Mr W. S. Haldane and a Mr James More, without a great deal of difficulty, managed to get agreement on all points by September, and a Bill was presented to Parliament for the 1901 Session. The terms reached with Falkirk included a wayleave payment of £40 per mile per annum, or £72 per annum if the Council undertook maintenance. For upkeep the promoters agreed £100 per mile per annum for five years, £120 thereafter. They also undertook to causeway the road from Carron Bridge to Camelon between the tracks and 18 inches either side. Outwith these boundaries the County Council settled for one row of setts on either side of the rails. Two crossings of the River Carron and two of the Forth and Clyde Canal were involved, and by agreement with the Caledonian Railway, who now owned the canal, new bridges were to be built for the tramways.

In 1901 the Falkirk and District Tramways Order Confirmation Act authorised:

Tramway No. 1.   6 chains double track; 9.4 chains single track, from New Market Street to Vicars Street.

Tramway No. 2.   7 chains double track; 3 chains single track, from tramway No. 1 to Grahams Road.

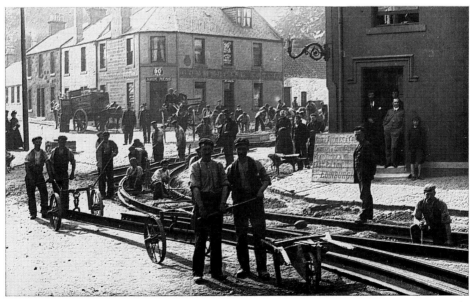

Construction of the triangular junction at Larbert Cross. It is quite noticeable that none of the large workforce is bareheaded.

7

The depot at Carmuirs under construction. The cars have arrived before building work is complete. Note how the upper deck panels are arranged for transporting.

Interested spectators — mostly children — watch for the cars carrying the official party, Grahams Road, 21st October 1905.

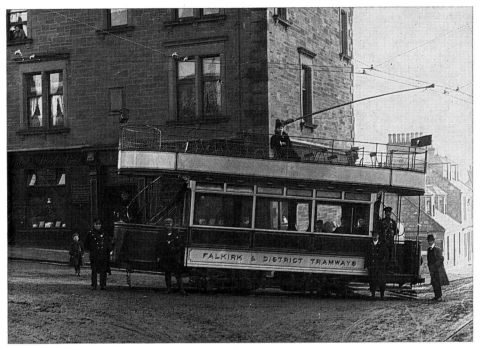

Car 17 posed at Larbert Cross, November 1905.

Tramway No. 3.	6 furlongs, 5.28 chains double track; 4 furlongs, 4.15 chains single track, from tramway No. 2 to centre line of the Carron bridge.
Tramway No. 4.	7 furlongs, 2.2 chains double track; 1 mile, 1 furlong, 1.16 chains single track, from tramway No. 3 to 110 feet north of N.E. corner of the building line at Larbert Cross Roads.
Tramway No. 5.	1.5 chains single track from tramway No. 4 to tramway No. 6.
Tramway No. 6.	1 furlong, 9.5 chains double track; 5 furlongs, 8 chains single track from tramway No. 4 (1.1 chains south of its termination) to Falkirk Burgh boundary at Camelon.
Tramway No. 7.	3 furlongs, 6.6 chains double track; 1 mile, 1 furlong, 0.5 chains single track from tramway No. 6 to New Market Street to connect with tramway No. 1.

The Act also included as Works Nos. 8 and 9, the reconstruction of Bainsford and Camelon Canal Bridges. The gauge was stipulated as 4ft 0in. Powers were granted to divert Tramway No. 2 from the existing Bridge over the railway at Grahamston on to any subsequent bridge. The Act did not go unopposed through its Parliamentary career, objections being lodged by various frontagers, and by the North British Railway relating to costs associated with the bridge at Grahamston, and the Caledonian Railway in respect of the canal bridges. These were all overcome and the Act received Royal assent on 2nd July 1901 (1 Edw. VII, c.xxxi). The Company had an authorised capital of £250,000 and eventually £96,260 was subscribed.

Of the four major bridges involved on the route, only one was fit to carry the tramway (that over the Carron near Larbert). In fact, to carry loads exceeding three tons across the canal bridges — which were wooden bascule type — prior notice had to be given and a barge was floated under and wedged up for additional support. On more than one occasion the load landed in the canal! The cost of these bridges proved an insurmountable obstacle to the tramway promoters, and Falkirk Town Council

9

Workers' cars leaving
Carron Works.

Car 11, Grahams Road.
Note the barefoot spectato

Crossing the old bridge ov
the River Carron, south of
Larbert

found it impossible to collect the agreed way-leave. In May 1904 however the scheme was revived and an "Edinburgh based Company" acquired a 6 months' option to purchase the powers of the Provisional Order. This "Edinburgh based Company" was in fact Messrs Bruce Peebles and Company, who had recently promoted the Scottish Central Electric Power Company and was then involved in the construction of a large generating station at Bonnybridge. The tramway would be a valuable customer.

Bruce Peebles was an electrical engineering firm, established at Pilton, near Edinburgh, in 1903 and they undertook tramway installations at Sunderland (District), Llandudno, Shanghai, Delhi and Athens. At the Pilton works there was an electric shunting locomotive which served as a "guinea-pig" for many of the Bruce Peebles traction motors and controllers.

Obviously the two original promoters were not agreed on the transfer of the Powers, as John More, who apparently was to have been Consulting Engineer to the tramways, attempted but failed in August to obtain interdict to block the deal. Bruce Peebles now approached the Town Council for permission to run cars on Sundays, and the Council agreed to consider this, but only after arrears of wayleave had been settled. After obtaining half the cash a plebescite of ratepayers was arranged which returned a 2097-1108 verdict in favour of Sunday cars. The Council after deliberation decided that cars must not disturb church services, and operation would cease from 11.30 to 12.30 and 2.15 to 3.15.

The next move was the incorporation on 24th October 1904 of a new Company, the "Falkirk Electric Construction Syndicate Ltd.", with an office at 37 Castle Street, Edinburgh, to acquire the rights under the Falkirk and District Tramways Order Confirmation Act of 1901. Capital amounted to £100,000 in 1,000 units of £100, of which 940 were allotted by 15th March 1905. The first action of this Company was to acquire the £96,260 of shares issued by the Falkirk and District Tramways Co., following which an order was placed with Bruce Peebles to the value of £81,000 for the construction and equipping of the tramway.

Construction

A speedy start was made, the first load of rails arriving during January 1905, and laying commenced shortly afterwards in both directions from Larbert Cross. Permanent way construction was sub-contracted to A. G. Whyte & Co. of London, but unfortunately the pace slackened in March, when a large number of men were paid off due to the non-arrival of whinstone paving setts. The track, to 4ft 0in gauge as authorised, was mostly single with twenty-one loops of varying length, and one stretch of double track in Grahams Road. Rails were 90lb/yard BSS No. 1 in 45ft lengths laid on a 6-inch thick bed of concrete. BSS No. 1C rails were used on curves, the sharpest of which was 48ft radius (35ft on the triangular access junction to the depot). Points, crossings and special work were of Hadfields "Era" manganese steel. The steepest gradient was 1 in 15.5.

Erection of the overhead commenced in May. This was of side bracket arm construction throughout except for three-quarters of a mile at Grahams Road, where span wires were used. Poles which were used in addition for lighting purposes were provided with bases made locally which contained the arc lamp resistances, switches, fuses, etc. Round copper 4/0 gauge trolley wire was used. Power supply to the trolley wire was divided into the usual half-mile sections.

The contract was well under way when a dispute over the sale of electricity nearly jeopardised the whole undertaking. The Construction Company had made an agreement with the Power Company for a supply at 1¼d per unit, but unfortunately they had no authority to supply power within the Burgh. The Council's rates for supply were considered outrageous by the Company who then appealed to the Board of Trade for a ruling. This body saw no reason to alter the power supply agreement and the Town Council thereupon decided to take the dispute to the Court of Session. However, early in October, after test runs had been made outwith the Burgh, agreement was reached whereby the Power Company paid £100, plus £30 per annum to the Burgh for the privilege of supplying the tramway power within the boundary.

Power was supplied from Bonnybridge Power Station at 3,300 volts A.C. to a substation adjoining the depot, where it was transformed to the usual traction current of 500 volts D.C. All the substation equipment was by Bruce Peebles and included an H.T. incoming switchboard with controls for two Peebles-la Cour motor convertors each of 200 kw nominal capacity. These motor convertors, it was claimed, scored heavily over the conventional rotary convertors on efficiency, capital cost and space requirements. They were wound twelve-phase and were thus stated to be much more stable in parallel than rotary convertors; also, the D.C. output could be varied by shunt regulation independently of the A.C. input. The equipment of the substation was completed by a low tension switchboard, negative booster panels, three main feeder panels and Board of Trade panel. The three positive feeders were of 3 sq in "Dialite" laid solid in wood troughing bitumen filled, and the feeding points were at Carmuirs, Falkirk Post Office and Carron. Negative feeder points were at Arnot Mill and Stenhousemuir.

Car 17 in New Market St before 1907.

French built car crossing Bainsford Canal Bridge. Note the special cantilever overhead post on left.

The major works in the Bruce Peebles contract were the rebuilding of the three bridges at Carron, Bainsford and Camelon. The first mentioned was over the River Carron, and a tripartite agreement was drawn up whereby the Carron Company gave £250 plus the old Wagon Road Bridge, Falkirk Burgh undertook the construction of the bridge towards which the Tramway Company gave £750, and the County Council granted rates rebates for two years. A further condition was that the Local Authorities would put no obstacles in the way of future tramway extensions to Grangemouth and Laurieston. Demolition of the old bridges started in June and the new structure was completed by September, at a cost of £3,850.

The two canal bridges were subcontracted, the steelwork to Motherwell Bridge Ltd., and electrical work to the Bridge Electric Equipment Co. of London. The agreement with the Caledonian Railway provided for the whole of the construction costs being borne by the Tramway Company, but maintenance charges would be divided equally. The bridges were designed to carry 16 tons, and had 16 foot wide roadway with single track tramway, plus a 5 foot footpath. That at Bainsford was 58ft 6in long, and that at Camelon 70ft long. They turned on rollers on a 7 foot diameter turntable on the bank, the overhang being compensated by a balance weight. Operation was by a 5 hp motor drawing a wire rope round pulleys, but a stand-by hand winch was provided. The overhead trolley wire was divided into three sections, two lengths of 100 yards on either side, plus the length which moved with the bridge, these sections being independently fed through a switchboard in the bridge-keeper's cabin. Four poles were mounted on the bridge, two at each end with corresponding poles on the bank, all of which supported curved girders in place of the customary span wire. These girders carried a mechanical device for aligning the trolley wire.

Operation of the bridge was fully interlocked to prevent any possibility of a car falling into the canal. Railway-type semaphore signals were set to "danger", gates were closed across the roadway, and these were inter-connected with catch points which were open to derail any car rolling forward by momentum. All three overhead feeders were connected through the top contact of a double throw switch which, when the bridge had to be turned, was moved to the lower position, thus disconnecting overhead power and connecting in the bridge-operating motor. This motor could be started (using a tramway-type controller) only after the bridge locking pins had been withdrawn. The full movement of the bridge took 55 seconds. As each bridge was opened on average 40 times per day, the disruptive effect on traffic was great.

The car depot was built on a plot of two acres in open country at Carmuirs, almost midway between Larbert and Camelon. The unpretentious building measured 130ft by 82ft, and in addition to six tracks for car storage, had a small workshop and various offices. Half length pits were provided on bays 1, 2 and 3 and a full length pit on bay 4 which extended into the workshop area. Bays 5 and 6 were shorter than the others, giving storage for 22 cars altogether.

Rolling Stock

The first batch of cars arrived on 19th July at Grangemouth Docks, shipped on the S.S. Dunavon from Dunkirk. A second shipment arrived early in August. The bodies were built in France, by the Compagnie Générale de Construction of St. Denis, by subcontract from Bruce Peebles. All fifteen were double-deck cars with extended canopies, 180° turn stairs and three arched-top windows to the saloon. The bodies were 28 feet long over the fenders and 6ft 6in wide over the waist panels. Longitudinal seating for 22 on varnished pitch-pine seats was provided inside, and garden seats for 28 outside. The interior woodwork was of polished walnut with oak doors and maple roof. Hudson and Bowring automatic life guards were fitted. Brakes were hand and rheostatic only. Destination boxes were above the upper deck decency boards. The livery of the cars was Prussian Blue for waist panel and dash, lined out in gold leaf, and cream lined out in dark blue or black for decency panels and rocker panel. The rocker panel lettering and the number on the dash were in gold shaded with blue and red. The truck and fenders were black. Dark green curtains were fitted to the saloon side windows, but were soon removed. Trolley heads were of the swivelling type.

Controllers, of the magnetic blow-out type, were manufactured by Bruce Peebles, and had four series, four parallel and six brake notches, with separate but interlocked main and reversing drums. The trucks supplied were of 6ft 0in wheelbase, of the 21E type, probably constructed under licence in France. Two 30 hp motors were fitted, supplied by Bruce Peebles, but probably built by Ganz & Co. of Budapest. These were stated to be a great improvement on those then in general use, and had bearing housings in separate castings from the cast steel motor cases. The armature bearing lubrication was also different from standard practice in that an oil-ring was used of a special shape to prevent noise.

Before the opening an order for three additional cars was placed with the Brush Electrical Engineering Company of Loughborough. These were of the same type, overall dimensions and seating capacity as the French cars, and were numbered 16-18. In appearance, however, they were quite dissimilar, having three flat-topped windows to the saloon, with opening quarterlights above. The side panels of the Brush cars were more curved than the French cars, and the dashes were lower. The saloon seats of the Brush cars were of cane. Cars 16-18 were mounted on Brush AA trucks with 6ft 6in wheel-base. It is believed that electrical equipment was identical with the other cars, i.e. Bruce Peebles "P.P.P." controllers and 30 hp Peebles-Ganz motors.

Opening and Route

The first trial run was made on 23rd September between Larbert and Camelon, and on 16th and 17th October a trial service was in operation to train crews. Since the lines had not been inspected, no fares were charged! On the 18th the Board of Trade's electrical advisor, Mr Trotter, approved the line. The following day Colonel Von Donop inspected and passed the trackwork and cars, fixing the speed limits and compulsory stops. The stage was now set for the opening ceremony, which was advertised for noon on Saturday 21st October.

At the appointed hour the Provost and Town Council embarked on their circular tour through streets lined with cheering children. Leaving the Burgh Buildings, they followed the line as it turned sharp left down the steep hill of Vicars Street, then over the railway at Grahamston Station by what was almost a hump-backed bridge. As double track the route continued down wide Grahams Road with, behind the houses on the left hand side, Grahamston and Burnbank Iron Works, and to the right Falkirk Etna Iron Works. Crossing the Canal Bridge the line entered Main Street, Bainsford, and ran as single track with two passing loops, then to a double track stretch over the new Carron Bridge and past the main entrance to the Carron Iron Works. Before the right angled bend the line singled, then crossed the Iron Company's railway on the level. There was a Board of Trade compulsory stop here, and conductors had to get off the car and walk to the corner to signal the all-clear to the driver. The line continued along the narrow twisting country road to Goshen, with one intermediate loop at Carron Dams. After Goshen, Stenhousemuir was reached and the line ran along Main Street with loops at the Plough Hotel and Burnhead, then came a short stretch of double track ending at the bridge over the Caledonian Railway at Larbert Station. The track became single along Main Street, Larbert with one loop before the Cross was reached. Here there was a triangular junction, with one line pointing towards Stirling but stopping after 25 yards. The purpose of this junction is not known, but it was included in the Act and therefore built. When the Bill was drawn up there were proposals afoot to electrify the venerable Stirling horse tramway and build extensions in all directions, including to Falkirk. It seems probable, therefore, that this junction was to connect up with the electrified Stirling tramways. Unfortunately — or perhaps fortunately for potential shareholders — the Stirling tramway remained as Scotland's last horse tramway until it closed in 1920 and the link was never made. As far as is known the triangle was not used for short workings, Larbert Station being the recognised part-way terminus. At the first re-laying of the curve the triangle was lifted. Leaving Larbert by Falkirk Road, the tramway passed through the narrow arch of the "stone bridge" under the Caledonian main line, and here Mr Trotter required boards to be fixed warning passengers not to touch the live wires which were carried low and to one side of the arch. These boards — albeit almost illegible — remain to this day. Immediately the line made a double bend to recross the River Carron, then continuing on the Edinburgh-Stirling turnpike road, to Camelon Station where it passed under two separate overbridges. Between the depot and Camelon was "One Tree Loop", so named after the isolated sycamore tree which still stands there. At Camelon one loop started under the railway and a second carried the track round yet another right angle into Main Street. From Camelon back to Falkirk was mostly built up, but after the second canal crossing was made the line ran between the high walls of Bantaskine House on the south and Darroch on the north. Public operation started after the official party had completed the circuit.

Unfortunately the arrangements were marred by a dispute with the Caledonian Railway, who refused to allow the trams to cross the canal bridges until alterations were made to overhead poles which obstructed the tow-path. These were the support poles for the mechanical overhead aligner, and eventually they were replaced by poles set behind the tow-path and carrying a large latticework cantilever for the overhead. However, until this was done the circle was incomplete, and for the first few months the line was worked in two distinct halves. Cars were supposed to connect on either side of the bridge but often failed to do so, causing great annoyance. Eventually the poles were repositioned but the circle proper was not instituted until 12th March 1906.

Special cars at Laurieston terminus, 3rd September 1909. The chief inspector is the uniformed figure in front of car 10, and Douglas Hays is in front of the car stairs, wearing a straw hat.

The two opening day sp
leaving Mary Square, La
showing car 18 with top

Car 3 near the "Skew" F
Laurieston. The old cott
have been demolished re

Laurieston terminus, c.1
Car 1 showing duty num
Driver Lamb and Condu
Fox.

16

Early Operation

The basic circular service was run by six cars, three in each direction. Large duty numbers were hung below the canopy, 1, 3 and 5 running anti-clockwise, and 2, 4 and 6 clockwise. A 15-minute frequency in each direction was given, 45 minutes being allowed per circuit. Part-day intermediate cars, duty numbers 7 upwards, ran from Larbert Station to Camelon Station via Falkirk to give a $7\frac{1}{2}$ minute peak frequency over this part of the route. These cars were known as the "Jerkers". Special workers' cars were run as an important part of the revenue earning activities and at the end of each shift at Carron Works four cars waited, two going in each direction. Unfortunately the Canal bridges greatly disrupted services and on occasions such as when the East Coast fishing fleet passed through at the beginning or end of the season the timetable was completely disorganised, the bridges being closed to road traffic for periods of up to an hour. In an attempt to improve punctuality, early in 1906 automatic signals were provided for all loops which were not intervisible. As a car entered the single line it lit a lamp at the loop it was approaching, warning on-coming traffic. This tended to reduce the number of head-on confrontations on single track.

From June 1906 the circle fare was reduced from 4d to 3d, with consequent increase in passengers. During the first full year's operation, over three and a half million passengers were carried, but the Company did not pay a dividend, declaring that the excessive wayleaves and bridge costs were taking all the profit.

The first manager, R. D. McCarter, came from a similar post with the Sunderland District Tramway Company. He was not short of ideas to promote the line, and in July 1906 emulated contemporary American practice by organising a Sacred Music Band recital in the grounds opposite the tram depot, with the Falkirk Military Band. Unfortunately his plan misfired, for instead of having to take a car to the end of the line (because the Falkirk line did not have an "end"), over 5,000 people appeared — mostly on foot! Another of his ideas was the Grand Children's Gala Day. On the first day of the school holidays, children under 12 were carried free provided they had persuaded an adult to take them. Crowds of boys gathered at stops to beg "lifts", and a thoroughly enjoyable day was had by all. The Gala was repeated a fortnight later, and became an annual institution until the First World War. A parcels service was started in August 1906. Conductors weighed parcels and fixed stamps. Stamps were also sold in books at a slight discount, the cost varying from 1d for a 7lb parcel to 6d for 1 cwt (the maximum).

During the early part of 1907 R. D. McCarter resigned, and Douglas Hays was appointed to the post which he filled very successfully for over twenty years. His previous experience had been gained with the British Westinghouse Company. He was not short of initiative either, and one of his first moves was to reorganise traffic during the annual Tryst Fair. The previous year, with every car pressed into service, serious delays had occurred, but on 8th, 9th and 10th September 1907 all cars ran anti-clockwise round the circle, i.e. from Falkirk via Bainsford, Carron, Larbert and Camelon, back to Falkirk. The great advantage of course was that there were no delays at loops, and it was hoped that although passengers would perhaps have to travel a greater distance, the greater speed would compensate. A simplified fare scheme was used, 1d for one stage, 2d for any distance beyond one stage, 3d for a complete circuit. A $2\frac{1}{2}$ minute frequency service was run successfully, and on one day over 26,000 passengers were carried, using 17 cars. The cars ran till midnight and the time for a circuit was reduced to 38 minutes.

Later in 1907 top covers were ordered from Hurst Nelson for fitting to cars 16-18. These had three side windows and canopies at each end. Headroom inside was 6ft 1in. They were fitted during March 1908 and greatly increased the carrying capacity in winter months when few passengers wished to brave the elements on an open-top car. To enable these cars to pass under the bridges at Camelon Station the roadway was lowered at the expense of the Tramway Company.

Mr Hays had intended to purchase additional top covers for the remaining cars, but after only three years' use the French built cars had already proved a very bad bargain and were not structurally sound enough to carry the additional weight. First to give serious trouble were the trucks, and in May 1908 an order was given to Hurst Nelson to supply "very urgently" fifteen standard H.N. 21E type trucks. This was followed a few weeks later by an order to supply and fit trusses to one car body and when this was done successfully the other fourteen were done likewise. New B.T.H. GE58 (30 hp) motors and controllers were supplied and the work was carried out by Hurst Nelson fitters, as it was so urgently required that the Company's small maintenance staff could not cope. Fortunately all this rebuilding was accomplished without affecting the service.

About this time a rail-grinder car was purchased. Little is known about it but it had a rectangular water tank and was also used as a snow plough. It was stated later to have equipment similar to the other cars, which would probably mean GE58 motors and B.T.H. controllers. This may have been supplied by Mountain and Gibson Ltd., who were at this time associated with Bruce Peebles. It is said to have carried number 19 and was painted brown.

After public agitation for $\frac{1}{2}$d fares, a new scale was introduced on 5th September 1908. The line was divided into twelve $\frac{1}{2}$d stages, but the minimum fare remained 1d. Over two stages (1d) the fare increased by $\frac{1}{2}$d for every stage up to six. For over six stages and up to a complete circuit, $3\frac{1}{2}$d was charged. Workers' fares were half ordinary fares. The fare stages were indicated by a broad white band with a red ring in the centre of the overhead pole, and were Gairdoch Street — John Street — Grahamston Station — Camelon Road (pole 281) — Camelon Road (pole 309) — Camelon Railway Station — Carmuirs Colliery — Larbert Viaduct — Larbert Station — Plough Hotel — Steps Road — Carronshore Road — Gairdoch Street. Children travelled any distance for 1d. Unfortunately this revision did not halt the downward trend in passenger figures, which dropped by nearly 30% to just over two million during 1909.

Expansion

Shortly after the opening of the circular route, negotiations were begun regarding extensions to Laurieston and Grangemouth. Agreement was reached and the Provisional Order was lodged early in 1906. One clause in the agreement gave Falkirk Town Council the use of any tramway in the burgh from midnight to 5.00 am for refuse disposal and road maintenance, with powers to build any connecting tramways found necessary. As one of their conditions, Grangemouth Town Council insisted that the line be carried to the eastern boundary through a completely unpopulated area. During 1906 the Falkirk and District Tramways (Extensions) Confirmation Act was passed which authorised the following lines:

Tramway No. 1.   3 furlongs, 5.6 chains double track; 1 mile, 9.4 chains single track from a connection with the existing tramway at west end High Street to Mary Square, Laurieston.

Tramway No. 1A.   7 chains double track; 2 furlongs, 9.4 chains single track from the termination of tramway No. 1 to Polmont Road, Laurieston.

Tramway No. 2.   1 mile, 1 furlong, 3.7 chains double track; 2 miles, 4.8 chains single track from a connection with the existing tramway at Vicars Street to the bridge over the Grange Burn.

Tramway No. 2A.   1.5 chains single track from a connection with the existing tramway at New Market Street to tramway No. 2.

Tramway No. 3.   1 furlong, 0.5 chains double track; 5 furlongs, 0.2 chains single track from the termination of tramway No. 2 to the Grangemouth Burgh Boundary in Bo'ness Road.

The Act also provided for widening Grangemouth Road between the Falkirk and Grangemouth boundaries from its then 16 feet to 40 feet.

After many further meetings the Tramway Company agreed to commence the Laurieston route on the following beneficial terms: (a) No wayleave payment to be made for three years: (b) During these three years the Company would maintain the streets: (c) Payment of £1,500 to be made to the Company, (i) £750 on commencement of work on Laurieston route, (ii) £750 on commencement of Grangemouth route, or 7 years after signing of agreement: (d) Tramway Company to widen the High Street at number 45: (e) Construction of the Laurieston line to start within three months. The Tramway Company also obtained agreement that cars would run for traffic only from Kirk Wynd to Laurieston and that the lines from Kirk Wynd to west end High Street would only be used to get cars to and from the depot. This being accepted, no rebuilding of the narrow streets was required.

Laurieston Branch

Construction of the first extension planned, that to Laurieston village, began in June 1909 and was completed by the end of August. The contractors were Messrs A. Stark of Glasgow, and in addition to the tramway construction they also paved the High Street at the Town Council's expense. From the east end of the High Street the track was not paved across, but only had a strip of setts on either side of the rails. Overhead work was undertaken by the British Insulated and Helsby Cable Company, and side bracket arms were used throughout except in the High Street, where wall rosettes were fixed. The major work was the lowering of the roadway under the "Skew Bridge" at Laurieston. Here the Company excavated and laid the track, and the roads were made up to the track level by the County Council.

A trial run was made on 30th August, and Von Donop — by now a Lieutenant-Colonel — inspected the line on 3rd September. After the official party had travelled the route, he expressed his satisfaction, the line opened forthwith, and he and the other guests retired to the Crown Hotel. Von Donop must have had a cast-iron construction, considering the number of railway and tramway functions he attended before his retiral in 1916. Speeds of up to 16 mph on the un-built up section of the line were authorised. This was considered very fast for a 4ft 0in gauge line with top-covered cars. The fare for the Laurieston line was 1½d any distance, with 1d single and 1½d returns for children and workers. Through tickets were issued, e.g. Laurieston — Larbert (4½ miles) 3½d single, workers and children 2d; Laurieston — Carron (3½

The Tramway Company bus fleet in April 1919. The vehicle nearest the camera is Commer No. 6 (originally No. 1). Then come Tilling Stevens Nos. 9, 10, 11, 7 and 8. The following five vehicles have been fitted with gas-burning apparatus.

"The Point", Stenhousemuir, in 1929. The dilapidated condition of car 6 is made more obvious when compared to Pender's new Thorneycroft bus.

miles) 2½d single, workers and children 1½d. The circle fare was reduced again, back to 3d, and long distance stages became 2½d with 4d returns, e.g. from Larbert Station to Falkirk Town Hall. It was advertised that on the new route the cars would run strictly to schedule (whereas the circle route tended to be quite irregular due to the interruptions at the Canal bridges) and clock faces were erected at Mary Square and Kirk Wynd where moveable hands were set to show the departure time of the next tram. A basic 20-minute frequency was given by one car, and it carried duty number 16. When a second car was used at peak periods to double the frequency, it had number 17 allocated.

From its connection with the existing tramway at Bridge Street, the new line immediately passed into the very narrow High Street. Double track was laid through the narrowest part with the outer rails almost in the gutter. It seems that normally only the northmost of these was used for runs to the depot. The High Street frontagers had raised great objections to the scheme, but only opposite No. 45 were road widenings required. This ratepayer made things awkward by not selling at an early stage, and for three months the track past his property was single. After he was bought out and the street widened, double track was substituted. The terminus was opposite Kirk Wynd, by the Steeple, in a fairly wide part of the street, but there were frequent complaints about the narrow part at Roberts Wynd being used as the turning place, causing obstruction. Just before the Burgh boundary the line shifted from the road centre to hard against the north side footpath. This was to gratify the whim of Mr Forbes of Callander Park, the high boundary wall of which occupied the south side of this road as far as the Skew Bridge. The aspect of this area has now changed radically. The estate wall has disappeared and the estate can now be enjoyed by all citizens of the burgh. Overhead poles were all on the north side. Outside the Burgh boundary the rails were laid on sleepers instead of the usual concrete base. This later caused increasing maintenance costs, and unending complaints about rough riding. The road surface was of water-bound macadam.

Car 12 passing the Depot in Larbert Road, 1929. The bright blue paint is now dull and faded.

Pre-War Period

The five-year time allowance for tramways authorised by the 1906 Order expired in 1911, so a further Order was promoted, obtaining its Confirmation Act in 1912, for the lines numbered 2, 2A and 3 in the 1906 Order. The powers for the extension past Laurieston were not revived, and it is extremely doubtful if the Company would have pursued Tramway No. 3 from Grangemouth to Bo'ness Road. In the new Act provision was made to alter the line of Tramway No. 2 over a bridge which had been built across the new Caledonian Railway goods line from Bainsford to Grangemouth. The length abandoned was 2 furlongs, 4.10 chains, replaced by 2 furlongs, 3.55 chains on the new alignment. However, an extraordinary general meeting of the Company in August 1912 decided not to increase the capital to finance any extension. The project was delayed "in the meantime", but was never revived.

A motor charabanc gave the first indications of the shape of things to come by challenging the Tramway Company's monopoly at the 1910 Tryst. The Company soon saw the possibilities of bus operation, and purchased a 25-seat Commer WP2 charabanc, registration LN9772, which was known as the "Grey Torpedo Car". The inaugural run was to Queensferry on 21st June 1913, and for this treat the fare was 2/-. A second Commer charabanc (with interchangeable lorry body), MS1176, was purchased in 1914 and they then were given fleet numbers 1 and 2 respectively, painted with huge figures on the radiator.

An Extraordinary General Meeting of shareholders in Edinburgh on 22nd May 1914 resolved to change the name of the Company from the Falkirk Electric Construction Syndicate Ltd. to the Falkirk and District Tramways Company Ltd.

War-time Operation

At the outbreak of the Great War the Tramway Company was in a good financial position. Dividends of 4% or 5% were paid annually after recovering from the expenditure of over £4,500 on the rolling stock repairs of 1908, and increasing annual passenger totals had passed the three million mark in 1911. Bus No. 2 was comman-

Brush bogie car No. 1 photographed in late 1930, with James Marshall's name newly painted in the corner of the rocker panel.

deered by the War Department, but during 1914, following easing of restrictions in petrol supply and the establishment of munition works in the area, an occasional service was commenced from Falkirk to Grangemouth. Following the arrival of a Tilling-Stevens petrol-electric bus (MS1348) a regular 40-minute frequency service was inaugurated on 1st January 1915 from Manor Street, Falkirk, to Charing Cross, Grangemouth.

Soon, due to the large number of employees enlisting, services were restricted, and in June 1915 the first "lady conductors" were employed. Of the pre-war total of 67 employees, only 38 remained with the Company a year later. After June 1916 women were employed as drivers also, and by 1918 there was an "Inspectress", Mrs Spicksey.

One of the few pieces of contemporary documentation still existing is an employee conduct register covering the period 1906-1917. Unfortunately only part is legible, but this gives fascinating insight into day-to-day working at that time.

Douglas Hays emphasised the need for economic running, and current consumption was his particular forte. In 1909 Falkirk took third place in the Scottish tramways' "power consumption league". The Falkirk figure was then 1.03 unit per car mile, while Dundee took bottom place with over 2.10. A tram driver's wage in 1915 was 5¾d per hour, rising after proven ability to 6¼d in two years. Unsatisfactory current consumption records led to a reduction in rate for a period. No obvious improvement could lead to dismissal. For driving downhill with power on, one week's reduction of wages was the standard punishment. Offences were many and varied, and punishment graded with demerit marks being allocated to each offence and accumulated until some drastic action was taken; failing to set the destination screen cost 10 marks, as did punching a ticket at the wrong stage; 20 demerit marks were given for each uncollected fare discovered by an inspector; for putting a car off the rails in New Market Street, Driver Inglis earned 50 demerit marks. A caution from the Chief Inspector was the next punishment, two cautions meaning dismissal. Offences which earned a caution included failing to observe Board of Trade stops and "allowing a strange boy to turn the trolley and destination sign". A period of suspension from duty could be imposed, e.g. one day for running the car with the trolley in the wrong direction, three days for smoking on duty, five days for running the car on to the dead section at an open Canal bridge and derailing at the runaway points. For the most heinous offences the ultimate sentence was dismissal, which was not often invoked. However, it was applied to one motorman who entered a public house whilst in uniform, and to Motorman Haxton who, in a hurry to get back to the depot to sign off, overtook another car going in the same direction at Camelon Station loop! The record does have its more humorous side, however, like the driver who resigned because he got wet one day; as his was one vocation where being wet and cold was the norm, he was obviously not cut out for this work. Or there was the conductress who received a caution for "playing about in the street with her driver"!

To help the war effort, in April 1918 the "Tramway Tombola" was started. This was a copy of a similar Glasgow scheme — a form of primitive Bingo. For a 1d ticket, sold by conductresses, a lucky number could win War Savings Certificates to the value of £200 for first prize. There were second, third and fourth prizes of £75, £50 and £25 respectively, and thirty consolation prizes of £5 and one hundred of £1. These draws were held monthly until the end of 1918, and at times over 125,000 tickets were sold in one month.

The standard of maintenance dropped drastically during the war, and deterioration in track conditions led to increasing complaints about the state of the system. The cars of course suffered, and in 1916 Hurst Nelson sent tradesmen to Falkirk to repair the bodywork of car 18, and the following year cars 17 and 16 were sent to Hurst Nelson's Motherwell works for more substantial repairs. (These cars were again open-toppers, as the top covers fitted in 1908 were removed c.1913 when they were sold to the Dumbarton Tramways, and fitted to cars 7, 8 and 21.) The work undertaken on car 17 included four new corner pillars, four new side pillars and stiffening plates on the headstocks, while the end cross bars of the frame required additional angle stiffeners, and the tops were straightened to give a level floor. New heavier truss rods were fitted, the platform steps were made horizontal, and "an attempt was to be made to take the lateral wind out of the frame". The treatment afforded to car 16 was to fit 4 new corner pillars, 3 new side pillars, new bottom light rails and guard rails; the frame was squared up with a new centre cross bar, and other cross bars straightened with steel angles. New truss rods and platform flooring were supplied and the doors were re-hung. There is no doubt that the limited workshop facilities in the depot had combined with the wartime shortage of men and materials to reduce these cars to such an appalling condition.

Hurst Nelson also supplied, in 1916-18, fifteen sets of dash plates, probably because the French ones had rusted through, and twelve staircases, presumably for the same reason. The new dashes were considerably lower than the originals, and quite altered the appearance of the cars. After this date very little maintenance, and certainly no repainting, was undertaken on the cars and their condition worsened until the once pristine bright blue paintwork had weathered to a dull grey-green, and delays occurred daily due to mechanical failures.

Despite all these drawbacks, however, the volume of traffic generated by the additional war work increased to a peak in 1919 when over five million passengers were carried. Shareholders benefited to the extent of a 7% dividend in that year. Many additional passengers travelled by hanging on to the ends of the cars — doubtless few of them paid fares — so to stop this practice, sloping metal shields were fitted over the fenders.

Post-War Competition

The end of the war saw the start of regular omnibus operation. A service from Redding to Falkirk commenced as early as September 1916 by the Linlithgow Motor Touring Co., using a 30-seat charabanc. Andrew Wright of Bainsford ran an Aster charabanc on various local routes, and in June 1918 Walter Alexander opened an hourly Sunday service, Falkirk-Denny-Bonnybridge-Falkirk, using an ex-army lorry which served as a charabanc on Sundays and reverted to goods carrying during the week. The Tramway Company increased their small fleet of buses and by 1918 was running a 15-minute frequency on the Grangemouth route. In February 1919 the route to Bo'ness was commenced, and a new large garage and workshop was built during the year, adjoining the tram depot in Larbert Road. The next service was Bannockburn-Bridge of Allan, inaugurated 11th September 1919, which helped to put the venerable Stirling horse trams off the road.

The railway strike of September proved the usefulness of the buses, when the Tramway Company ran emergency services as far afield as Glasgow and Edinburgh.

In December 1919 the formation was announced of a new Company to promote and run the omnibus side of the Tramway Company. This was considered necessary at this time to develop satisfactorily the expanding bus department. The Order of 1906 gave powers to the Tramway Company to run buses, but only in connection with the tramways, and for no distance greater than five miles from the tramway. A separate Company would overcome these difficulties. The new Scottish General Omnibus Company shared the Registered office of the Tramway Company, and Douglas Hays managed both undertakings. The SGO Co. was in fact registered on 10th February, but the proposals took until December to formulate. The vesting date was back-dated to 16th August, and the following vehicles were transferred from Tramway Company ownership:

1.	MS 1348	Tilling Stevens bus (42 hp)	Dec. 1914
2.	MS 1354	Tilling Stevens bus	Jan. 1915
3–5.	MS 1895–7	Tilling Stevens bus	Mar. 1918

6.	LN 9772	Commer charabanc (formerly No. 1)	June 1913
7–8.	MS 2018–9	Tilling Stevens bus (TS3)	Mar. 1919
9–11.	MS 2020–2	Tilling Stevens charabanc	Mar. 1919
12.	MS 2188	Tilling Stevens bus	July 1919
13–22.	MS 2230–9	Tilling Stevens bus	Aug. 1919

It is thought that MS 2239 was the first to be painted in "General" livery. Most bus bodies were supplied by Thomas Tilling Ltd., but some were by Christopher Dodson Ltd. of Willesden. The charabanc bodies were by Tilling.

Bus competition with the tramway reached a peak in the twenties, and some details of the large number of operators in the Falkirk area at this period are given in Appendix II.

As will be readily appreciated, cut-throat competition was rife, and with worn-out track and equipment the tramway carried fewer and fewer passengers each year. This situation could well have been the prelude to closure of the line, had not control of the Company (including the S.G.O. Co.) been acquired in April 1920 by the Fife Tramway, Light and Power Company, which was allied to the Balfour-Beatty group. The F.T.L. & P. Co. was incorporated in July 1909 to construct the Dunfermline & District Tramways and take over the Fife Electric Power Co., whose Townhill Power Station fed these tramways.

It became obvious that the policy adopted by the F.T.L. & P. Co. was one where the tramways played a substantial part of the transport scene, and capital was made

The motors of the new bogie trucks were mounted longitudinally and the worm drive gear is also shown in this photograph.

available for improvement works, both at Dunfermline and Falkirk. The bus side of the undertaking was not neglected, however, and the S.G.O. Co. continued to flourish under its new owners, who soon added to the Dunfermline tramways an Omnibus Department which was in effect an extension of the S.G.O. Co., and relied to a large extent on its workshop and managerial resources.

In 1920 a Confirmation Act was put through Parliament to empower the Tramway Company to increase the level of fares, which provision had not been included in any of the previous Acts. Under the new fare scale, the circular fare became 5d, with shorter stage fares proportionately increased.

Track Reconstruction

A start was made on major road reconstruction and track renewal schemes in 1921, the first section tackled being Camelon Road, from Camelon Canal Bridge to County Buildings, at a cost of £12,700. This work attracted a 50% Government unemployment alleviation grant. Much of the track was relaid as double and the road widened in many places. The following year saw the relaying of Main Street, Bainsford, and the widening of the roadway and re-alignment of the tramway at Falkirk Sheriff Court House. New Market Street was reconstructed in 1923, and there was a further fare increase, the minimum now 1½d, the circle 6d, and intermediate fares of 2d and 4d only. All road works so far undertaken were accomplished without affecting the tram service, but when the next section was undertaken, from Carron level crossing by Goshen to Steps Road, arrangements were made for complete occupation of the road, and the tram service was curtailed to become Carron-Falkirk-Steps Road. The reconstructed road, incorporating much longer sections of double track, was opened on 9th July, when the next section of the road westwards was closed and the trams ran Steps Road-Carron-Falkirk-Larbert Station only.

Following intensive bus competition a decision was made to abandon the Laurieston section rather than re-lay the worn out track. Trams ceased on 20th July 1924, the replacing S.G.O. bus service starting on Monday 21st. Agreement was reached for the Local Authorities to lift the track, this being completed by the end of the year.

A legal action to recover increased costs incurred in operating the two canal bridges since rebuilding was raised in 1924 by the L.M.S. The 1905 agreement stated that maintenance charges were to be split equally, but the Tramways disputed that the claim, for £5,130 in respect of additional staff now required, constituted a charge on maintenance. It was stated in evidence before the Railway and Canal Commissioners that prior to the rebuilding, one man looked after each bridge on a 24-hour basis, at a wage of 15/- per week plus 1d for each night boat between 10 pm and 5 am, but since then it had been necessary to employ further five men, working 8-hour shifts, at 42/- each per week plus 2d per night boat. Perhaps not surprisingly the Commissioners found for the Railway Company, and the Tramways appeal to the Court of Session had the same result.

Track reconstruction continued, and in 1925 the section from Larbert Cross to Camelon was undertaken, and from 31st August the tram service became Larbert Cross-Falkirk-Carron-Camelon Station. All road traffic to the north was diverted via Carron, and the opportunity was taken to divert the tramway across a new reinforced-concrete bridge over the River Carron at Larbert Meal Mill. This avoided the narrow bridge and double bend of the earlier route. One track was of necessity always kept open to allow cars access to the depot. The road was re-opened early in April 1926, but the old bridge continued in use until June, when the replacement was completed. At this stage the basic service was of 15-minute frequency between 6.15 am and 11.15 pm. On weekdays this was increased to 8 minutes between 11.30 am and 8.40 pm, and on Saturdays a 6-minute service was given from noon until the last car. The Sunday service was, first car 12.10 pm, then every 12 minutes to 4 pm, then every 8 minutes until the last car, at 10.10 pm.

Car 8 stops in Falkirk Road, Larbert, to pick up a lady passenger.

Car 2 photographed crossing the new bridge over the Carron at Larbert.

The 1926 General Strike caused a stoppage of all traffic. Afterwards the Company offered ex-employees their jobs back on the conditions pertaining prior to the strike, but met with a refusal to re-start without instruction direct from Union headquarters. The Company thereupon withdrew their offer and announced fresh terms of re-engagement, dropping drivers' rates by 1d per hour and conductresses' by $\frac{1}{2}$d. A further strike was threatened, but eventually agreement was reached and work re-started on the original conditions.

With the rebuilding of Stirling Road in July 1926, half the circle had been completed, and the time for the circuit was reduced when it was re-opened in August. New light signals were fixed to regulate traffic over single track sections, and this also assisted the speed-up. An announcement was made in the press that it was the intention of the directors to introduce new "Pullman" single deck trams as soon as possible and scrap the veterans then running. Even the manager described the cars as "derelict"! The new cars were planned to be 40 feet long but in the event the sharp curves of the route restricted the length to 29 feet. At this stage they were intended to have front entrances.

Track reconstruction continued, Main Street, Camelon, being tackled in 1926-7. In the summer of 1927 Grahams Road was the scene, and was closed to all traffic from 11th July to mid-September. The trams ran from New Market Street-Camelon-Larbert-Bainsford Bridge. Work was also undertaken at this time on the canal bridges, new signals were installed and automatic gates. Within 18 months the remaining track, in Vicars Street and at Carron had been rebuilt, and the circle completed.

Passenger journeys suffered a sharp decline during the reconstruction period, and early in 1926 fares were reduced in an endeavour to improve matters. In 1927 a dividend of 3% was paid to shareholders (mostly based on bus profits). From 1.5 million Falkirk tram journeys in 1928, the figure leapt to 3.3 million in 1931, following restoration of circular running and the introduction of the "Pullman" cars.

Financial Reorganisation

At an Extraordinary General Meeting of the F.T.L. & P. Co. in July 1929, agreement was reached on the sale of the complete electrical supply side of the undertaking to the Scottish General Power Company for £1,325,000, including the generating stations at Bonnybridge and Townhill. The F.T.L. & P. Co. remained in control of the Falkirk Tramways, Dunfermline Tramways, Scottish General Omnibus Company and Dunfermline Tramways (Omnibus department), with 64 trams and over 300 buses. Since its incorporation in 1919 the S.G.O. Co. had absorbed (amongst others) the Stirling & Bridge of Allan Tramway Co. in 1920; T. & J. Cousin (Culross) in 1925; The Comfort Bus Company in 1927; Crerar (Crieff) — including the 62 feet long M.V. "Queen of Loch Earn" — and Morris of Polmont in 1928; Dunsire's Motor Service of Falkirk, and Penman (Bannockburn) in 1929; and by 1930 with its associated companies operated throughout an area stretching from Glasgow to Bo'ness and St. Andrews, and also between Aberdeen and Inverness through the subsidiary Scottish General (Northern) Omnibus Co. Ltd.

The second depot, photographed in 1934, with cars 9, 10 and 1.

This state of affairs did not last for long, however, as the Railways Act of 1929 permitted the railway companies to acquire omnibus interests, and their controlling company, the Scottish Motor Traction Company, purchased the bus subsidiaries of the F.T.L. & P. Co. plus the Balfour Beatty bus interests allied to the Wemyss Tramways. Operation was vested from June 1930 in the S.G.O. Co.'s arch rival, W. Alexander & Sons Ltd., who had themselves been purchased by the railway interests the previous year. Within twelve months services had been re-organised and rationalised to avoid competition, and the ubiquitous blue Alexander's bus ruled the roost in what had been one of the most intensively fought-over bus arenas of the 1920s. Without the 1929 Act, things might have ended very differently.

Reverting to the tramway side, in 1929 the Company applied for a Provisional Order — perhaps with tongue in cheek — to regulate bus competition by giving them sole rights along the route already occupied while the tramway service was adequate — to restrict hours of opening the Canal Bridges (It was stated in evidence that while in 1913, 11,499 vessels used the canal, in 1928 this was reduced to 3,175 vessels, and that the canal was now closed on Sundays) — to give unlimited powers to run buses, and to alter the Company title from "Tramways" to "Transport". Similar Provisional Orders were lodged by seven other Scottish Tramways at this time, and all were opposed by local authorities and the railway companies (who were anxious to protect their bus interests). As a result of this concerted opposition the original Order was not proved, and only very restricted powers obtained. These allowed only the change of title and the requested bus powers.

The event of 1929 was the appearance of the "Pullman" cars. On 23rd August the first to arrive was tried out and made a great impression. It was placed in service on the 28th, and was soon followed by three more. Further six placed in service during 1930 completed the batch. These cars were numbered 1-10. They were built by the Brush Electrical Engineering Co. of Loughborough, and were long, modern, completely enclosed single deck vehicles. The saloons had longitudinal seating for 15 per side, in red moquette upholstered seats with shaped backrests. Four heating radiators were fixed under the seats. The cars were mounted on Brush maximum traction trucks with 27 inch diameter leading wheels and 4ft 0in wheelbase. Roller bearings were used throughout and the 35 hp motors were mounted in a "fore-and-aft" manner, driving by worm gears to the axle. Controllers were by British Thomson-Houston Ltd. To complete the transformation a new bright red and white livery was adopted, similar to that used by the S.G.O. Co., with lining out in gold leaf. Each cost £1,900.

While the first four cars ran interspersed with the old cars, it was not unknown for passengers to let one or two of these pass, and wait for a "Pullman" car! After delivery of the six additional cars the double deckers were gradually scrapped. It is believed four remained at the end of 1930 and the last one was scrapped about February 1932. The rail-grinder (car 19) appears to have disappeared about this time, having been seldom used latterly and spending most of its time rusting at the back of the depot.

Managerial Changes

In April 1930 Douglas Hays, having given over twenty years to the expansion of the Company and having seen the reconstruction and re-equipping of the Tramway, was promoted to manage the transport undertakings belonging to the Midland Counties Electric Supply Co. Ltd. This Company, also in the Balfour Beatty group, controlled the Notts. & Derby, Ilkeston, and Mansfield tramways.

As an interim measure Edward Nolan of the S.G.O. Co. assumed the managership of the Traction Company. Mr Nolan had worked from 1906 to 1919 on the trams, as conductor, inspector, then traffic superintendent. He transferred to the S.G.O. Co. in the same capacity, and eventually was traffic manager for all Scotland. On his retiral

Four-wheeled car No. 11, second hand from the Dearne Tramways, emphasising the "home-made" appearance of this particular car.

in July 1930, James P. Marshall was appointed to the managership. A native of Cowdenbeath, Mr Marshall had been advertising and tour manager for the S.G.O. Co., then for four years was assistant manager of the Dunfermline trams.

A reorganisation of the bus facilities at Larbert Road in 1931, with garaging centralised on the old S.G.O. base, and repair work transferred to Alexander's original Brown Street premises, moved the trams into a new depot away from the bus complex. This consisted of a four-track building with workshop facilities at the rear and offices adjacent. It was situated north of the old depot, towards Larbert.

In January 1931 the Traction Company exercised their new powers to run buses when they acquired one of the remaining competitors, Pender. The ten buses continued running on the same route, but were operated (still in Pender's colours) by Alexander on behalf of the Traction Company. A 1d increase was made on all ex-Pender fares to protect tramway interests.

Further four new trams were added to the fleet in August 1931. These were also by Brush and were similar to the original ten. The only external distinguishing feature was the provision of an air intake louvre at the back of the dash opposite the platform, to help cool the resistances. Internally, however, transverse (two and one) seating was provided. The corner seats over the sandboxes remained. All seats were fully upholstered, but the capacity was reduced from 30 to 28. These new cars took numbers 13-16, implying two old cars numbered 11 and 12 remained. It is doubtful if these would be the original cars of these numbers, but there is now no evidence available to give any further information. The basic service was now a car every 15 minutes before 1 pm, every $7\frac{1}{2}$ minutes thereafter. At weekends after 4 pm a 6-minute frequency was given, requiring twelve cars.

Additional Cars

In September 1933 the Dearne District Light Railway Company closed and its 30 nine year old trams were offered for sale. These were all single deckers, built by the English Electric Co., with two DK30B motors of 30 hp. Anly nine cars found further use, four with the tramways of Lytham St. Anne's Corporation, and five with the Falkirk & District Traction Company.

Major rebuilding was required, for both truck and body, and it was not until early 1934 that the first car entered service. Because these cars were four-wheeled with a long overhang, they would have been unable to negotiate the many sharp corners of the Falkirk circle, and the bodies were shortened from 32ft 0in to 28ft 9in. This was done by moving the saloon bulkheads at each end inwards, producing a home-made looking arrangement, with three large windows flanked by two small ones. The Peckham trucks were re-gauged from 4ft 8½in to 4ft 0in, and shortened from 8ft 6in wheelbase to 7ft 4in by removing 1ft 2in from the middle and bolting the ends together. The track brakes were removed from all trucks except one.

None of the five cars, after rebuilding, was identical to any other, each having its own peculiarities. Four Dearne cars had been modernised with cross-seating, and as four of the five at Falkirk had this feature, it seems reasonable to assume these four modernised cars came north. The cross-seat cars became 11, 12, 17 and 18, but the corner sand-box seats of these cars, in contrast to the Brush cars, were not upholstered. Car 11 had a rebuilt vestibule, with three equal sized front windows, quite a flat appearance, and an upward sweep to the roof above the windscreen, whereas the others retained basically the Dearne vestibule with the roof line carried level at the ends. Car 12 had the truck which retained the mechanical track-brakes, and it is alleged that this car doubled as a rail grinder car with carborundum blocks in place of brake blocks. It is known that it spent much of its life parked on the siding which was laid outside the depot to accommodate the increased fleet. 17, 18 and 19 were similar, but the vestibules had variations. 19 had longitudinal upholstered seating for 26, and the other cars seated 23. The front exits on these cars were retained for a short time but not used, and were soon blocked off. It is not known who undertook the fairly major rebuilding, but it may have been done in the tramway workshops. The Dearne cars, whilst retaining that Company's red and white livery, were repainted after reconstruction, and in the process lost all of their former owners' elaborate lining out. They appeared in unrelieved livery, with the new owners' title and manager in minute lettering on the corner of the rocker panel. The Brush cars, at their first repaint, also lost all lining out. The bogie cars soon had large advertisement panels mounted on the sides and ends of their roofs, completely ruining their fine lines, but the "ugly sisters", the Dearne cars, never carried advertisements.

Final Years

The future of the tramway now seemed secure, and it was ready to fill an important part in the transport scene of the area, with modernised track in smooth asphalted roads and trams which were capable of 35 mph. The poorest circle service became a car every ten minutes, increased to five minutes after lunch time, and at week-ends to four minutes. Every year saw an increasing number of passenger journeys, reaching a peak of 3,776,319 in 1934. However, early in 1935 an approach was made to the F.T.L. & P. Co. by S.M.T., who offered shareholders 3/9d for each 5/- share, giving a cash value of £281,250 for the tramways in Falkirk and Dunfermline. The Directors recommended acceptance and by June, 99.2% of shares had been purchased. An immediate announcement was made that the line would close, ostensibly to relieve the new owner (controlled by the railway authorities) of the responsibility of bearing part of the cost of maintaining the canal swing bridges (also controlled by the railway authorities). A more likely explanation is that as the tramways had attracted back the traffic they had lost, and were now quite profitable, they were seen as an impediment to the "rationalisation" of the omnibus services.

During 1936 negotiations were entered into with the local authorities to arrive at terms for track lifting, and as soon as agreement was reached, closure arrangements were finalised. Falkirk Town Council were paid £5,500 plus the value of the rails, while the County Council accepted £805 per mile, plus £750 and the rails.

Events moved swiftly now, and with very little excitement the last tram was taken into the depot by Inspector A. Walton who had driven one of the first cars on the opening day, thirty-one years before. A floral wreath was hung over the headlight. The date the journey started was 21st July 1936, but it was completed after midnight, on the following day!

The cars, all very modern by tramway standards, indeed some only five years old, were all sold off by September, fetching only about £50 each. Perhaps the 4ft 0in gauge deterred any other tramway from purchasing them, but they could easily have been re-gauged and could have given many years' valuable service. They might even have found a home in Wellington (New Zealand) which was then an expanding 4ft 0in gauge system, but this was not to be. A number became holiday caravans at Carron Valley Reservoir, and one Dearne car came to rest at Plains, near Airdrie. The second life of these cars was considerably longer than the first, but as far as is known, none remains in existence now. Dismantling of overhead work was commenced immediately, and rails were lifted quickly, starting with Main Street, Bainsford, in August. Since, on reconstruction, the track had been bedded in concrete up the web, the head of the rail only was cut off, and the bases of the rails remain to this day over much of the route.

Tangible evidence today of the tramways is difficult to find. The two depots remain, with a short length of rail still in the original building — now part of Alexander's Larbert Road garage. The circular route is still followed by bus route No. 70. The frequency is now fifteen minutes basic, and the circular fare 22p (4s 5d). The trams have been gone forty years, but the service they gave has not been forgotten.

The final chapter in the history of the Company was written when the winding up meeting was held on 7th November 1943.

Ex-Dearne car No. 12 at the depot in 1935.
Note track brake and differing vestibule details.

APPENDIX I.

Fares and Tickets

Despite the essentially simple circular route, with its one branch, fare collection on the tramways was quite involved. Few tickets survive and therefore it is not possible to give much information on this side of the undertaking.

It appears that all tickets were purchased from the Bell Punch Company until T.I.M.s were introduced in 1933. All surviving tickets are of the fully geographical type.

The first issue, in 1906, was of 1d, 2d, 3d and 4d values, all white, with an overprint, in varied colour, of the denomination. Two arrows were also overprinted, to signify direction of travel. That on the left pointed downwards, that on the right upwards.

In addition to the single fares above, returns were issued, also children's and workmen's tickets.

Soon the circular fare was reduced to 3d, and at this time prepaid books of twenty-five tickets were available for 1d, 2d or 3d stages — but not at any discount.

Prepaid tokens were also used. These were metallic with a monogram of the Company initials on one side. The reverse was blank.

In 1908 halfpenny stages were introduced, although the minimum fare remained 1d. Tickets of 1d, 1½d, 2d, 2½d, 3d or 3½d were in use for single journeys, children were charged 1d any distance, and workers' fares were 1d and 1½d.

The opening of the Laurieston branch in 1909 brought further complications. The branch fare was 1½d single, with workers' and children's fares of 1d single, 1½d return, but in addition, special through booking tickets were issued, from Laurieston to Larbert 3½d single (worker or child 2d), or to Carron 2½d single (worker or child 1½d). Further return fares were available, e.g. Falkirk-Lambert 4d return (worker or child 1½d).

After powers were obtained in 1920 to raise fares, the intermediate ½d stages vanished, and the circle fare became first 5d, then 6d. New "popular" fares were introduced in 1923 and remained at the 1d per mile level thereafter. By this time the tickets were printed on coloured card, as is more usual practice, and colours used included 1d white, 1½d orange and 3d purple.

First issue 1d ticket.
(Red on white)

APPENDIX II.

Early Local Bus Operators

    i.   Walter Alexander (already mentioned) by 1920 was running over 20 buses on various local routes. In 1929, owned 150 buses.

   ii.   William Blaylock, Falkirk, commenced October 1928 with one bus running Dollar Avenue-High Station via High Street. Three buses by June 1931 when new route High Street-Dawson Park opened. Taken over by Alexander October 1937.

  iii.   Camelon Transport Co. were running local services and tours by July 1922, and commenced a five times daily run to Denny from Hope Street on 5th May 1923.

  iv.   Thomas Cowie of Bonnybridge ran between there and Falkirk, c.1922.

   v.   Dunsires Motor Services Ltd. (originally Magnus Dunsire), Bainsford, commenced tour operation early in 1925, and opened a route Hamilton Street (Camelon) — Ladymill on 19th September 1925. Further services were introduced, Hamilton Street to Grangemouth on 20th March 1926, and to Larbert soon after. Taken over by S.G.O. Co., 1929.

  vi.   Erskine Motor Services (James Balnaves), "several buses" at June 1931, no further details known.

 vii.   A. F. Gordon, Bo'ness, by December 1929 was using five buses on the Falkirk-Grangemouth-Bo'ness run.

viii.   Grangemouth Motor Service Co., running Grangemouth to Glasgow in January 1921 using an Albion bus, also Grangemouth-Manor Street, Falkirk from July 1920.

  ix.   Grant's Motor Service, in operation 1930.

   x.   Douglas Hasten, Falkirk, was operating tours in 1925.

  xi.   Laird & Morrison of Grangemouth ran McFarlane Crescent-Grangemouth in 1920.

 xii.   Linlithgow Motor Touring Co., running 30-seat charabanc between Falkirk and Redding, started on 2nd September 1916.

xiii.   Malley of Bainsford toured with two charabancs (14 and 16 seats) from 1926.

xiv.   William Mason of Camelon operated Hope Street-Grangemouth (?) in 1921, and Falkirk-Denny by 1922, with a "pre-war Albion".

 xv.   W. McKnight operated a "wagonette", Falkirk-Bonnybridge, Denny and Larbert in 1920.

xvi.   J. Monteith of Bainsford used a 14-seat charabanc for tours from 1926.

xvii.   Morris of Linlithgow (?) ran a service Falkirk-Polmont-Linlithgow in 1923.

xviii.   Hugh Pender of Rumford opened a service to Maddiston on 1st July 1922, then to Grangemouth later the same year. A Camelon-Bainsford-Larbert route competing with the trams over most of its journey commenced on 25th August 1923, a Lime Road-Larbert run in 1924 (?) and Larbert-Blackness in 1926. Three buses were owned in 1922, increasing to sixteen by 1929. The original 8d fare to Maddiston was reduced, after S.G.O. Co. competition, to $2\frac{1}{2}$d.

xix.   William Scott, New Market Street, used Lancia coaches for touring, but was acquired by Alexander in September 1933.

 xx.   D. Shields of Laurieston started as a horse bus proprietor c.1892, but by 1925 was running omnibuses from Falkirk to Laurieston and Grangemouth. He was bought out by Alexander in December 1930.

xxi.   Messrs Wilson, Marshall & Co., of Avonbridge, using the fleet name "Venture Bus Co.", ran Falkirk-Bathgate from 1928, also Falkirk-Airdrie. Nineteen buses owned in 1919. Acquired by Alexander in March 1930.

xxii.   Andrew Wright of Bainsford had a charabanc for touring in 1915, and subsequently opened a route from Falkirk to Blackness on 28th July 1923.

Source Material

Cadell: The Story of the Forth.

Dendy Marshall: History of British Railways down to the year 1830.

Lindsay: The Canals of Scotland.

Pratt: Scottish Canals and Waterways.

Town Council of Falkirk Burgh, Council Minutes.

Falkirk Herald.

Falkirk Mail.

Falkirk and District Almanack and Directory.

Edinburgh Courant.

Board of Trade Annual Returns.

Garcke's Manual of Electrical Undertakings.

Light Railway and Tramway Journal.

Modern Transport.

Tramway and Railway World.

Relevant Acts of Parliament and associated Deposited Plans.

Commer charabanc No. 2, MS 1176.
The number on the radiator can just be distinguished.

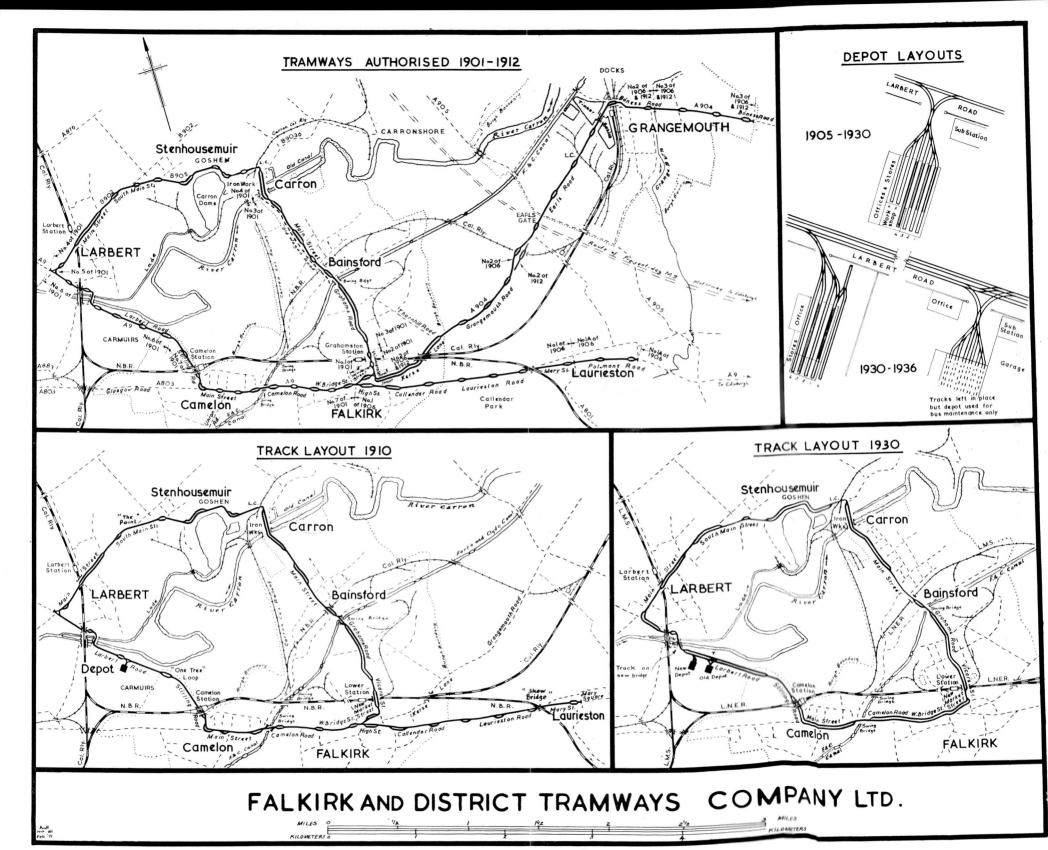

TRAMWAYS AUTHORISED 1901-1912

DEPOT LAYOUTS

1905-1930

1930-1936

Tracks left in place but depot used for bus maintenance only

TRACK LAYOUT 1910

TRACK LAYOUT 1930

FALKIRK AND DISTRICT TRAMWAYS COMPANY LTD.

MILES 0   ½   1   1½   2   2½   3 MILES

KILOMETERS 0   1   2   3   4 KILOMETERS